GREAT OUTDOORS
SPORTS ZONE

BIG GAME
HUNTING
BEAR, DEER, ELK, SHEEP, AND MORE

Tom Carpenter

Lerner Publications Company • Minneapolis

Lerner Publications Company
A division of Lerner Publishing Group, Inc.
241 First Avenue North
Minneapolis, MN 55401 U.S.A.

Website address: www.lernerbooks.com

Content Consultant: James G. Dickson, PhD, wildlife biologist, researcher, author, professor, and hunter

Library of Congress Cataloging-in-Publication Data

Carpenter, Tom, 1962-
    Big game hunting : bear, deer, elk, sheep, and more / by Tom Carpenter.
   p. cm. — (Great outdoors sports zone)
    Includes index.
    ISBN 978–1–4677–0222–5 (lib. bdg. : alk. paper)
    1. Big game hunting — Juvenile literature. I. Title.
 SK35.5.C37 2013
 799.2'6—dc23   2012004461

Manufactured in the United States of America
1 – CG – 7/15/12

The images in this book are used with the permission of: Backgrounds: © Dagmara Ponikiewska/Shutterstock Images; © xiver/Shutterstock Images; © Nebojsa S/Shutterstock Images; © FloraStyle/Shutterstock Images; © abrakadabra/Shutterstock Images; © Vule/Shutterstock Images; © Nate A./Shutterstock Images, p. 5; © North Wind/North Wind Picture Archives, p. 7; © Library of Congress, pp. 8 (LC-USZ62-55602), 9 (top, LC-USZ62-105065), 9 (bottom, LC-USZC4-11548); © Tony Campbell/Shutterstock Images, p. 10; © Mike Vivion/USFWS, p. 11; © John and Karen Hollingsworth/USFWS, p. 12; © Jean-Edouard Rozey/Shutterstock Images, p. 13; © USFWS, p. 14; © LSqrd42/Shutterstock Images, p. 15; © Nathan McClunie/iStockphoto, p. 16; © Jason Lugo/iStockphoto, p. 17; © Justin Kral/Shutterstock Images, p. 18; © Jason Lindsey/Alamy, p. 19 (top); © Keith Publicover/Shutterstock Images, p. 19 (bottom); © Dennis Steen/Shutterstock Images, p. 20 (top); © Jim Mone/AP Images, p. 20 (bottom); © s-eyerkaufer/Shutterstock Images, p. 21; © Nathan McClunie/iStockphoto, p. 22; © Rafa Irusta/Shutterstock Images, p. 23; © Donna Lorka/iStockphoto, p. 24 (top); © June Scheffel/Shutterstock Images, pp. 24–25; © Red Line Editorial, p. 25 (top); © reidBETH/Shutterstock Images, p. 26 (top); © Ryan Hagerty/USFWS, pp. 26 (middle), 27 (bottom middle); © Karen Laubenstein/USFWS, pp. 26 (bottom), 27 (top middle); © Gary M. Stolz/USFWS, p. 27 (top); © Steve Hillebrand/USFWS, p. 27 (bottom); © Lee Avison/Shutterstock Images, p. 28; © Margo Harrison/Shutterstock Images, p. 29 (top); © Petr Jilek/Shutterstock Images, p. 29 (bottom). Front cover: © Mark Kayser/Windigo Images.

Main body text set in Avenir LT Std 65 Medium 11/17.
Typeface provided by Adobe Systems.

TABLE OF CONTENTS

CHAPTER ONE

WHY GO BIG GAME HUNTING?

Deer, bears, elk, moose, and bighorn sheep are all big game. These animals live in the mountains, forests, and prairies across the United States and Canada. These animals can be tough to find. But it is worth the hard work. Just sighting one of these animals can be thrilling. If you're looking for adventure, it's hard to beat big game hunting.

Part of the fun is getting ready for your hunt. You may need to travel to a faraway place. You need to line up gear, get your bow or firearm ready, scout out your hunting spot, and study hunting tactics.

Hunting big game can take you to beautiful places. It can be a great way to spend time outdoors with an older friend or family member. Big game also taste great. The meat from your harvest will feed your family for a long time. Every big game animal you shoot is a trophy to be proud of. Take plenty of pictures. Bucks, bulls, and rams (males) have antlers or horns that many hunters want to keep as trophies.

Big game hunting is a thrilling sport that takes place in the woods, fields, and mountains across North America.

CHAPTER TWO

HISTORY OF BIG GAME HUNTING

Native Americans were the first big game hunters in North America. Before European settlers arrived, Native Americans had a lot of game to hunt. White-tailed deer were common. Elk and black bears lived in the mountains and forests. The plains were full of pronghorns, elk, mule deer, white-tailed deer, and especially bison. Native Americans relied on these animals to feed and provide for their families.

BISON

Native Americans sometimes hunted bison by trying to drive the herd. They lit prairie fires or formed large human lines behind a herd of bison. This pushed the animals toward hunters waiting with bows and arrows. Sometimes hunters would drive the animals off cliffs. When the Spanish brought horses to the Great Plains in the 1500s, bison hunting changed. A hunter would ride alongside a speeding bison, draw the bow, and send an arrow into the animal's chest. By the late 1800s, some Native Americans used guns. Native American hunting did not threaten bison populations. But settler hunting did.

Native Americans disguised themselves with animal skins to get closer to bison herds.

Native Americans hunted using a variety of methods. In eastern woodlands, they hunted with bows and arrows. Some Native Americans draped animal skins over themselves as a disguise so they could get closer to game. Sometimes they would find a deer trail and hide beside it until a deer came along. Native Americans didn't just use the meat of big game. They made clothing and shelter out of animal skins. They used the bones, antlers, and horns for tools.

As settlers expanded west across North America, they hunted bison almost to extinction (none left alive).

Europeans Arrive

European settlers started arriving in North America in the 1500s. Later, they spread west across the continent in great numbers. Settlers cut down trees and cleared prairies for farming, houses, and cities. This took away big game habitats (living spaces). Settlers hunted with rifles. Some hunted lots of game and sold the game to city markets. Soon big game animals were being killed at a faster rate than they could reproduce. Big game populations began to drop.

By the late 1800s, it was rare to see a white-tailed deer. Elk were scarce. Mule deer only lived in secluded mountains. Bison had almost become extinct (died out completely). People started taking action to protect big game and other animals.

Conservation, or the smart use of natural resources, was born. People set up conservation agencies to protect wildlife of all kinds.

President Theodore Roosevelt was a hunter. He helped establish a system of national parks and public lands. These were protected lands where big animals could live and be seen without being hunted. Big game populations started to increase again.

Thanks to modern game management and strong conservation efforts, white-tailed deer are abundant. Pronghorns number over a million, and elk over six million. Bison populations have come back from the edge of extinction to number around 200,000 bison across North America. Black bears also are expanding their range and can be hunted in some states.

President Roosevelt was one of many conservationists who worked to protect wildlife.

CHAPTER THREE

PROTECTING BIG GAME

Big game animals need good habitats for hiding, finding food, raising young, and surviving winter. Every species has different habitat needs. White-tailed deer thrive in brushy areas mixed with fields. Mule deer prefer open countryside. Bears need big, wild areas. Elk live in remote mountain forests and meadows. Sheep like high mountain areas.

The number of animals a habitat can support is called its carrying capacity. Sometimes the animal population can grow to be greater than the land's carrying capacity. That happens when healthy and plentiful habitats are available.

White-tailed deer are the most common big game animal. They like areas with low plants and bushes, but they can live almost anywhere.

A biologist studies a black bear sleeping in its den.

The responsibility of managing game populations and habitat falls to state fish and game agencies. Every U.S. state and Canadian province has a fish and game agency to manage wildlife.

Hunting Seasons and Bag Limits

Biologists are scientists who study living things. They work with fish and game agencies to set hunting seasons and bag limits for big game. These rules make sure hunters don't hurt big game populations by taking too many animals in a habitat.

Bag limits are laws about how much game a hunter can shoot each season. A hunter may be limited to shooting one deer, elk, or bear in a season. Most big game hunting seasons take place in the fall or winter.

Hunting Licenses

All big game hunters need to buy a hunting license. Hunting license sales support game departments and their work. The money from licenses helps protect big game and their habitats. Some licenses for certain types of big game can be hard to get because so few licenses are issued. In some states, hunters may have to enter a lottery to get a black bear license. In other states, black bears are a protected species and cannot be hunted at all.

Different states have different hunting rules. It may be legal to hunt a big game animal in some states but illegal in a neighboring state. Learn your state's rules before you hit the hunting grounds.

Bucks and Bulls vs. Does and Cows

During most hunting seasons, male deer, elk, and moose have antlers on their heads. With this, it is possible to tell males and females apart. Pay attention to the antlers. Wild sheep have permanent horns. The males' horns are bigger than the females. Some licenses are restricted to bucks, bulls, or rams. Does, cows, and ewes (females) are sometimes protected so they can keep having offspring. Other times, when big game populations need trimming, hunters can shoot doe deer or cow elk. Know what game you are licensed to shoot before you start hunting.

Antlers make great trophies for a hunter. They also help you know if the elk you are shooting at is male or female.

CHAPTER FOUR

BEING A SAFE HUNTER

Hunting is a big responsibility. You must know how to use firearms safely. You must buy a hunting license. Know and follow all hunting rules and regulations.

Safety Training

Most states require young hunters to take firearms or hunting safety courses. In these classes, you will learn how to use a firearm safely.

Places to Hunt

All state game agencies list public hunting lands on their websites. These public lands include wildlife management

A firearms safety class will help you learn how to handle guns safely and responsibly.

Whether you are hunting on public or private land, make sure big game hunting is permitted and allowed at the place you are going.

areas; refuges; and county, state, and national forests. Never hunt on land if you're not sure it's legal to do so in that area.

Big game hunters often hunt on private land. Private farmland is especially good for white-tailed deer. Ask permission to hunt on private land. Show the landowner you are a responsible hunter. And thank the landowner after hunting. That way, the land could be yours to use in the future too!

FIREARMS SAFETY

Here is the basic formula for gun safety. Remember these letters: TAB-K.

- Treat every firearm as if it were loaded.
- Always point the muzzle (tip of the gun) in a safe direction.
- Be sure of your target and what lies beyond.
- Keep on the safety (a device that prevents accidental firing), and keep your finger off the trigger until you are ready to fire.

BLAZE ORANGE

Blaze-orange clothing helps prevent hunting accidents. It is required during most rifle or shotgun seasons for big game. Even if it is not the law, wearing blaze orange is a good idea. Blaze orange is like no other color in nature. It helps you spot other hunters and avoid confusing them with big game. This color also helps other hunters see you clearly, keeping you safe.

Blaze-orange clothing helps this girl stand out from nature.

Hunting Regulations

As a hunter, you need to learn and follow all hunting regulations. Not knowing the law is not an excuse for breaking it! You can find regulations booklets at sporting goods stores, state offices, or online.

Key regulations to know include the following:

 Hunting season dates: Make sure hunting season is open.

 Shooting times: Good light is needed for shooting. Find out when it is legal to shoot in the morning and how late shooting is allowed in the evening.

 Bag limits: Know if you can shoot male or female game and how many animals you can shoot.

 Tagging rules: You usually have to attach a tag (part of your license) to an animal after shooting it.

Part of hunting big game responsibly means taking careful shots. If you're not sure you can hit an animal well enough to take it down, don't shoot at it.

Fair Chase

Good hunters follow a code of ethics beyond what's in a regulations booklet. Acting ethically means doing the right thing, even when no one is watching. This means hunting in a way that is fair to animals and other hunters.

Good ethics include hunting with fair chase methods. Never drive around in a vehicle looking for animals. Work hard to find the game you shoot. Shoot only if you feel confident you can hit the animal and take it down. Make the most of your game meat. These are just a few examples of ethical hunting.

CHAPTER FIVE

LET'S GO HUNTING!

It's almost time to go hunting. But remember, big game hunting is challenging. Big game animals are smart and careful. You have to be ready. You need the right equipment, effective hunting strategies, and good hunting skills.

Rifles

Center-fire rifles are powerful, long-range firearms that can hit game animals that are as far away as 300 yards (270 meters). But closer is better. A scope mounted on your rifle will help you aim and shoot more accurately. If you can, rest your rifle on a rock or a stand to keep it steady.

A center-fire rifle is a good tool for hunting big game. Rest your rifle on a stand or other rest to keep it steady.

Shotguns

In some areas where farms or homes are nearby, only shotguns are allowed for hunting. Their range is not as far as that of rifles. Shotguns for big game shoot rifle slugs (solid lead bullets). Shotguns can be accurate to as far away as 100 yards (90 m).

Archery Gear

Some hunters choose to hunt big game using bows and arrows. This type of hunting can be very challenging but fun. It's exciting getting close to a big game animal to shoot. The season for bow hunting often starts earlier and ends later than rifle season. Modern arrows are tipped with broadheads (sharp, bladed points) for hunting.

A compound bow has a pulley-and-wheel system that lets you hold the bow at full draw (all the way back) more easily. Some hunters use old-fashioned longbows similar to what Native Americans used. Other hunters use a more modern recurve bow, which is a little less bulky.

Compound bow

Riflescope

Optics

Good optics (sighting equipment) are important for big game hunting. Binoculars and spotting scopes magnify your view so you can spot game better and see details, such as antlers. Riflescopes can be mounted to firearms, helping you aim with more accuracy.

Clothes

Big game hunting can take you into all kinds of weather conditions. Wear clothes suited to the extreme temperatures where you are hunting. Wool is a good material because of its warmth. Fleece is also warm. Both materials allow you to move quietly.

Boots and Socks

Sturdy hunting boots are important to keep your feet warm and comfortable while hunting. Wear hiking boots in milder weather and warm boots with thermal liners in cold weather. Wear warm socks made of material that will help keep your feet dry.

Wear comfortable clothes and shoes when big game hunting.

Stands

Big game hunters often use stands when hunting. Stands are elevated platforms where a hunter can wait for big game to come near. When a deer or a bear wanders by, the hunter is in position to shoot. A stand might be its own structure or might attach to an existing tree.

Stand safety is very important. Never hunt in a homemade tree stand. Use commercially made and approved tree stands and follow all setup instructions. Never climb in or out of a stand with your firearm. Leave it unloaded on the ground. Then pull it up with a rope. When you leave the stand, unload your firearm before lowering it down. Follow similar rules with a bow and arrows. Always wear an approved safety harness when climbing, sitting in your stand, and coming down.

A stand gives you a bird's-eye view of the surrounding area.

Hunting Skills

Your equipment is ready to go, so it's time to go hunting. No matter which hunting strategies you use, the following hunting skills are important for success:

 Wind in your face: Big game animals can easily smell you. When hunting, move with the wind blowing in your face. This means your scent is not blowing toward animals in front of you.

 Look hard: You must spot game before it spots you. Don't look for entire animals. Look for pieces: a leg, an ear, the horizontal line of an animal's back, or the glint of sun off an antler.

 Listen carefully: Be quiet so game doesn't hear you. Being quiet also means you can hear game. You may hear the crunch of leaves as a deer walks, the grunt of a buck, or the call of an elk.

Keep a sharp eye for big game. These animals are often shy and will avoid people if they spot them.

Still Hunting

When still hunting, move very slowly through an area where game may be. Stop, look, and listen more than you walk. Try to spot game before it spots you.

Stand Hunting

When stand hunting, you will pick out one spot where you will wait for game to appear. You may wait beside a deer trail that the animals use to move to feeding fields. You also may wait in a tree stand.

If you heard a loud bugling sound, an elk may be nearby.

To be a good spot-and-stalk hunter like this woman, you need to be slyer than the animal you are hunting.

Spot-and-Stalk Hunting

In this technique, you will use your optics equipment to spot game. Figure out the animal's location or path of travel. Then stalk (sneak) into position for a shot. Spot-and-stalk hunting takes good eyes.

Baiting

In many states, black bears are baited with food with a strong odor, such as meat or greasy food. It is left in a location that a bear might visit. Baiting is hard work. You have to keep bringing bait back so the bears keep coming. Then stand hunt near your bait and try to shoot the bear. Check the baiting laws in your state.

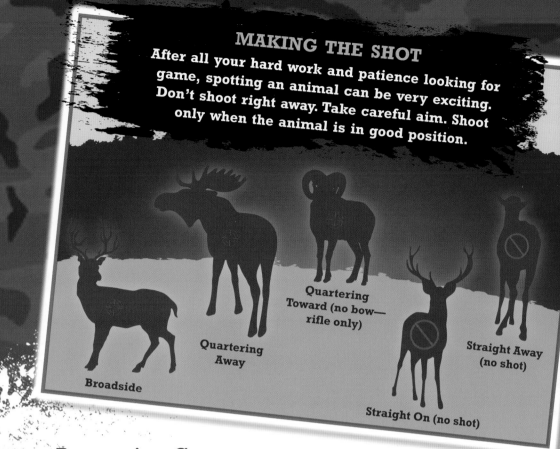

MAKING THE SHOT

After all your hard work and patience looking for game, spotting an animal can be very exciting. Don't shoot right away. Take careful aim. Shoot only when the animal is in good position.

Quartering Toward (no bow— rifle only)

Quartering Away

Broadside

Straight Away (no shot)

Straight On (no shot)

Recovering Game

Big game animals are strong. They don't always fall at the spot you shoot them, especially if you are using a bow and arrow. They will often run away after being shot. You sometimes need to trail the animal to recover it. Look for pieces of hair and blood at the place you shot the animal. Then look for signs where the animal might have run. You might see knocked-down brush or broken branches. This trail will lead you to your animal.

Where legal, baiting is a good way to attract black bears.

BIG GAME GUIDE

MULE DEER

Mule deer live in dry, open country in western North America. Mule deer habitat can be deserts, prairies, foothills, mountains, and ranch country. An adult mule deer can range from 140 pounds (63 kilograms) to 200 pounds (90 kg) or more. Spotting and stalking is a good way to hunt mule deer in the wide-open country they prefer.

WHITE-TAILED DEER

White-tailed deer live in forests, prairies, mountains, and farmland across North America. An average deer can be as small as 80 pounds (36 kg) in the South or as large as 225 pounds (102 kg) in Canada. The best way to hunt whitetails is to stand hunt. Sit quietly and perfectly still, waiting for a deer to move into range.

ELK

Elk live in the mountains and foothills of western North America, where they feed in grassy meadows. Elk are big. They can weigh from 250 pounds (113 kg) to more than 1,000 pounds (454 kg). To hunt elk, you can wait at a likely feeding area. Still hunting through wooded areas or spot-and-stalk hunting in open areas also works well.

BLACK BEAR

Black bears usually live in wild, forested areas. Black bears are omnivores, meaning they eat plants as well as meat. Black bears weigh from 150 pounds (68 kg) to 600 pounds (272 kg). Where legal, baiting bears is the best way to hunt them. In the mountains, you can sometimes spot-and-stalk bears.

MOOSE

Moose are huge. They can stand almost 7 feet (2.1 m) tall at the shoulder and weigh from 400 pounds (181 kg) to more than 1,800 pounds (817 kg). Moose live in the far northern United States, most of Canada, and all of Alaska. A fun way to hunt moose is to canoe along a river or lakeshore looking for animals. Spot-and-stalk hunting also works.

BIGHORN SHEEP

Bighorn sheep live in desert and mountain areas. They also like rocks and meadows. Bighorns are strong, muscular animals. Their weights range from 120 pounds (54 kg) to 300 pounds (136 kg). Spot-and-stalk hunting is the best way to hunt bighorns. It might take all day to find one.

PRONGHORN

Pronghorns like wide-open, treeless plains and prairies. They weigh from 80 pounds (36 kg) to 150 pounds (68 kg). Pronghorns can run 50 miles (80 kilometers) per hour or more in bursts of speed. Spot-and-stalk hunting or still hunting are good techniques in pronghorn country.

27

BIG GAME CARE AND COOKING

🦌 Field Dressing

Because most hunters eat what they shoot, it's important to field dress (remove the internal organs) of the animal right away. This helps the meat cool down so it doesn't spoil. Always work with an experienced adult to field dress your game. Doing this step incorrectly or waiting too long can lead to meat that is unsafe to eat. With any processing, it is also important to keep the meat as clean as possible.

Once your animal is field dressed, store it in a cool place until it is time to process it or take it to the butcher. A butcher skins and cuts up your animal. Then the butcher turns the meat into steaks, chops,

ADULT HELP NEEDED!

Because you'll be using a sharp knife and working with raw meat, get help from an experienced hunter when you are field dressing and cooking big game.

A butcher can turn your hard-earned big game meat into delicious brats.

roasts, stew meat, hamburger, or sausage. Whatever you are hungry for! Most butchers can process your meat within a week or two. Some experienced hunters prefer to butcher and prepare their own big game meat.

Big game animals have a lot of meat. If you have more meat than you want to take home, many butchers will donate the extra meat to a local food shelf or charity. For an extra fee, many butchers will return the animal's hide (skin) to you. Big game hunters often keep antlers or horns as trophies of their success in the field.

Cooking Big Game

The best cooking methods for big game are fast, on high heat (so the meat won't dry out) or slow, on low heat (to break down the meat and keep it juicy). A butcher can make burgers, summer sausage, meat snacks, breakfast sausage, brats, wieners, and other delights from your game meat.

One great way to cook big game is in a pot roast. Roll the meat in flour, brown it in oil in a skillet, and remove. Sauté two sliced onions and place the sautéed slices in the bottom of a baking pan, with the meat on top. Add 2 cups of beef broth, cover with foil, and bake in a 350° F (175° C) oven for 3 to 4 hours. Add chopped potatoes and carrots during the last hour.

After all that hunting, you're bound to be hungry. Fortunately, big game meat is delicious!

GLOSSARY

ABUNDANT

in large numbers

BAG LIMIT

the maximum number of animals of a species a hunter can kill in a season

BAIT

to put food out to attract animals, such as black bears

CARRYING CAPACITY

the number of animals an area of land can support

CONSERVATION

the thoughtful, efficient, and careful use of natural resources

ETHICS

the way a hunter acts in the field that is fair to the animals and the sport

HABITAT

the place in which an animal lives that provides the animal with hiding, food sources, and water

LOTTERY

a drawing hunters can enter to win the opportunity to buy a hunting license for big game

MENTOR

an experienced adult who helps a new hunter learn to hunt

NATURAL RESOURCES

things found in nature that are useful for humans

RANGE

the distance a firearm can shoot

FOR MORE INFORMATION

Further Reading

Berman, Ruth. *American Bison*. Minneapolis: Lerner Publications Company, 2009.

MacRae, Sloan. *Deer Hunting*. New York: PowerKids Press, 2011.

Sonneborn, Liz. *The Shoshones*. Minneapolis: Lerner Publications Company, 2007.

Swain, Gwenyth. *Theodore Roosevelt*. Minneapolis: Lerner Publications Company, 2005.

Websites

Junior Shooters
http://www.juniorshooters.net/
This website features information on hunting clubs, events, and safety geared toward young shooters.

National Geographic
http://animals.nationalgeographic.com/animals/mammals/elk/
Learn more about elk and listen to an elk call. Do a little more digging on the website to learn about other big game animals.

U.S. Fish and Wildlife Service: Hunting
http://www.fws.gov/hunting/
This website has information on conservation, national hunting regulations, and resources on where to go to learn the hunting rules for your own state.

INDEX

About the Author

Tom Carpenter has hunted and fished across North America for almost five decades, pursuing big game, waterfowl, upland birds, wild turkeys, small game, and fish of all kinds. He has raised three sons as sportsmen and written countless articles and contributed to dozens of books on hunting, fishing, nature, and the outdoors.